An Eye on Spiders

Black Widows

by Jenna Lee Gleisner

Bullfrog Books

Ideas for Parents and Teachers

Bullfrog Books let children practice reading informational text at the earliest reading levels. Repetition, familiar words, and photo labels support early readers.

Before Reading

• Discuss the cover photo. What does it tell them?

• Look at the picture glossary together. Read and discuss the words.

Read the Book

• "Walk" through the book and look at the photos. Let the child ask questions. Point out the photo labels.

• Read the book to the child, or have him or her read independently.

After Reading

• Prompt the child to think more. Ask: Have you ever seen a black widow? What more would you like to learn about them?

Bullfrog Books are published by Jump!
5357 Penn Avenue South
Minneapolis, MN 55419
www.jumplibrary.com

Library of Congress Cataloging-in-Publication Data

Names: Gleisner, Jenna Lee, author.
Title: Black widows / by Jenna Lee Gleisner.
Description: Bullfrog books.
Minneapolis, MN: Jump!, Inc., 2018.
Series: An eye on spiders | Includes index.
Identifiers: LCCN 2017040224 (print)
LCCN 2017047372 (ebook)
ISBN 9781624967894 (ebook)
ISBN 9781624967887 (hardcover : alk. paper)
Subjects: LCSH: Black widow spider—Juvenile literature.
Classification: LCC QL458.42.T54 (ebook)
LCC QL458.42.T54 G54 2018 (print) | DDC 595.4/4—dc23
LC record available at https://lccn.loc.gov/2017040224

Editor: Kristine Spanier
Book Designer: Molly Ballanger

Photo Credits: Jacob Hamblin/Shutterstock, cover; Peter Waters/Shutterstock, 1, 24; Robynrg/Shutterstock, 3; Moonborne/Adobe, 4; Snowleopard1/Getty, 5; John Serrao/Science Source, 6–7; Eric Isselee/Shutterstock, 8; Jeff March/Alamy, 9, 23br; Buddy Mays/Alamy, 10–11, 23bl; Joseph Berger/Flickr, 12–13; Stuart Wilson/Science Source, 14, 23tl; Daniel Heuclin/NHPA/Photoshot, 15; Visuals Unlimited, Inc./Jeff Howe/Getty, 16–17; James H. Robinson/Science Source, 18–19, 23tr; Meister Photos/Shutterstock, 20–21, 22.

Printed in the United States of America at Corporate Graphics in North Mankato, Minnesota.

Table of Contents

Black and Red

A black widow hangs in her web.

She is upside down.

See her belly?
It has a mark.

mark

Her body is black.
But the mark is red.
What does it mean?
Stay away!

Here comes a grasshopper.
It lands on her web.

Quick!
She bites it.
Venom turns
it to liquid.

Her back legs have hairs.

They cover it.

In what? Silk.

hairs

silk

Time to eat!

She sucks it up. Yum!

Males are smaller.
They are brown.

male

They mate.
Then she eats him!

15

She lays her eggs.
They are in a sac.
It is made of silk.

sac

spiderling

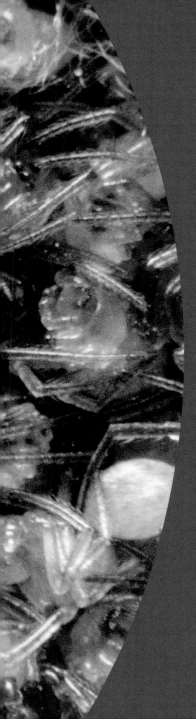

The babies are white.

They have a special name.

Spiderlings.

They leave.

They spin their own webs.

Where in the World?

Black widows are found in areas with mild temperatures throughout the world, including the United States, southern Europe and Asia, Australia, Africa, and much of South America.

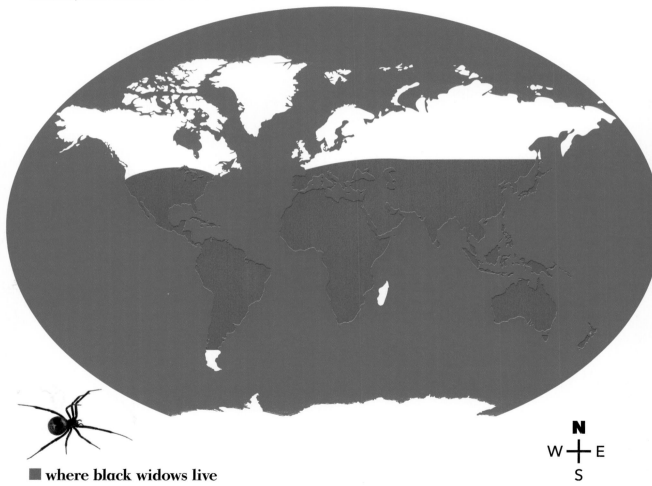

■ where black widows live

N
W ✛ E
S

Picture Glossary

mate
To come together and breed to make babies.

spiderlings
Baby spiders.

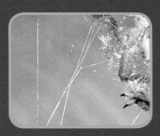

silk
Fine fibers spiders make to build webs or nests.

venom
A poisonous substance spiders inject to kill prey.

Index

To Learn More

Learning more is as easy as 1, 2, 3.

1) Go to www.factsurfer.com

2) Enter "blackwidows" into the search box.

3) Click the "Surf" button to see a list of websites.

With factsurfer.com, finding more information is just a click away.